THE DAY-BREAKERS

·THE DAY·

BREAKERS

MICHAEL FRASER

BIBLIOASIS
WINDSOR, ONTARIO

FIRST EDITION

10 9 8 7 6 5 4 3 2 1

Library and Archives Canada Cataloguing in Publication

Title: The day-breakers / Michael Fraser.
Names: Fraser, Michael, 1969– author.
Description: Poems.
Identifiers: Canadiana (print) 20210314532 | Canadiana (ebook) 20210314540 | ISBN 9781771964838 (softcover) | ISBN 9781771964845 (ebook)
Subjects: LCSH: United States—History—Civil War, 1861-1865—Participation, African American—Poetry. | LCSH: African American soldiers—History—19th century—Poetry. | CSH: Black Canadian soldiers—United States—History—19th century—Poetry.
Classification: LCC PS8561.R2978 D39 2022 | DDC C811/.6—dc23

Edited by Luke Hathaway
Copyedited by John Sweet
Text and cover designed by Ingrid Paulson

Cover image: City Point, Virginia. Negro soldier guarding 12-pdr. Napoleon. Model ?. United States, 1865. Photograph.

Published with the generous assistance of the Canada Council for the Arts, which last year invested $153 million to bring the arts to Canadians throughout the country, and the financial support of the Government of Canada. Biblioasis also acknowledges the support of the Ontario Arts Council (OAC), an agency of the Government of Ontario, which last year funded 1,709 individual artists and 1,078 organizations in 204 communities across Ontario, for a total of $52.1 million, and the contribution of the Government of Ontario through the Ontario Book Publishing Tax Credit and Ontario Creates.

PRINTED AND BOUND IN CANADA

MIX
Paper
FSC
www.fsc.org   FSC® C100212

Printed by Imprimerie Gauvin
Gatineau, Québec

Dedicated to all the African-Canadians who fought and died for the ultimate cause, freedom.

CONTENTS

The Day-Breakers / 9

COMES THE WORD / 11
Proclamation / 13
Henry Williams, 14 Years Old / 14
John Woods / 16
Soldier's Camp / 17
Frances Jane Scroggins Brown / 18
Thomas Arthur Brown / 19
Outside Chatham / 21
Readville / 22
Cornelius King / 23
Goshen / 24
Waiting / 25
Buckle Down / 28
Chaplain / 29
Puckerbrush Run / 30
Camp Ward / 31

33 / CLATTERING

35 / *African Canadian in Union Blue*

38 / *The Crater*

40 / *No Quarter*

41 / *Water Rippet*

43 / *Fort Pillow Massacre*

45 / *Grand Junction*

47 / *New York Draft Riots*

50 / *Latching Blackbirds*

52 / *Blockade*

53 / *Intruder in the Dust*

54 / *Captured*

55 / Hamilton Evening News

56 / *French Leave*

58 / *The Foragers*

60 / *Richmond*

62 / *Taking Charleston*

63 / *Fort Wagner*

INTO THE BONEYARD / 65

Andersonville Prison / 67

Field Camp / 68

William Fields / 69

Mary Fields / 70

And There She Ministers / 71

Banner / 73

The Black Union Dead / 74

Aftermath / 75

Go Down Moses / 76

George M. Lucas / 79

Burial Duty / 81

Consumption / 83

Breakfast / 84

James Jones / 85

Theatre / 86

Glossary / 87

Acknowledgements / 94

About the Author / 96

THE DAY-BREAKERS

We are not come to wage a strife
With swords upon this hill,
It is not wise to waste the life
Against a stubborn will.
Yet would we die as some have done.
Beating a way for the rising sun.

—Arna Bontemps

COMES
THE WORD

PROCLAMATION

Master Lincoln's words flutter horse-back
manes and snow-bogged train rails, dust
down sled-flow paths, and squall ice-weathered

snow walkways, they yellow backcountry dragsaw
cut sheds, slide past frosted knotwood log-bucks,
crow through windblown cow pounds, smooth

rhythmic church-clap songs, they break the
call-answer chirking of women stooped over ribbed
washboards, pounding barrels hem-topped with

wood-flamed boiled water. He's ignited fresh negro
hantles to pop-call recruiters and line-in for promised
bounties, their hopes following full-chisel fast flatcars

south to the ball's entrance, their blue-dudded frames
eager to wopse four centuries scrogged to scrimy hell,
their lives rail-rolling to new metaphors.

They took me by the blindside,
asked in for help loading stoneboats.
I coonjined decking logs then set the

tumpline down, removing sliver spikes
from my log-brushed hempshirt.
One shiner and a redhead set into me.

Of course I can read I says, and I
revealed the bible page he furnished
clear as the lord had placed the words.

His smile drummed the air and he
produced poke-bag paper, wanting to
know if I could quill my name. Then

they asked me again, now suspicion bit into
my idea-pot. Their eyes glazed fire, brows
haired-up, insisting I had orders to follow.

I was now soldiered, bonded to march or
face the coward's cage. Mama tried to stop
the subterfuge devised against me, tried

the charity of higher-ups who were too
weak to lift my signature. We couldn't force
time back up its hill or make the river return

to its shy spring source. Whenever I glim
my backstick past, I know that woods-queer
moment was devilish, more engineering than

blind chance. They whooked and trimmed me,
clunked me with adult fists. One day, I'll snap
back, and rip them like a forked plot hound.

JOHN WOODS

I crossed over and enlisted in Detroit,
recall the river eyeing me as
I left behind trilliums and saw the water
wash my reflection in a torrent.
They jawboned I'd shoe pelter horses.
I took the toll and they furnished me with
a musket, and I was regimented.
I marched blare-eyed, crocked,
my idea-pot half-knurled.
I was bug-dust to them,
a pinch ant, tangle-gut weed. Each morning,
I tried to grab the sky's overhung eaves,
hoping my sinewed bones would remain
to nourish this blight-snapped earth.

SOLDIER'S CAMP

In the peek space
between tent flaps,
the dust dawn light shakes
snowdrop flowers.

I draw a long face toting
stones for the rock fence,
see them hunched down
in the alder crest,
cannon men scarfing
the scrub cattle with
stone-sharpened cutters
the shorthorns' bloody innards
slathering buckshot soil.

The sky smoke is
hunger's body language
breathing, the flames
gather in more space.
We all watch hawk-eyed,
waiting for the meat
to be tuned up
and fire-played.

I card raw wool and think I see
him abeam through the window.
He walks the path upholding a
black bumbershoot in this
gulley-washer rain. I look again
and only see the sky's draggy
waterfall cutting the tag alders
and stump fence from sight.
My mind's at the end of its row.
The mooing swoo lean one way
against the free stall. I ribble off
our saviour's words, know he'll
provide larder to fill the root
house. I told my oldest he must
deacon skills his father knows.
The glim brightens this room,
lets the daylight down and furnishes
these brush-arbor walls. I need to turn
the batts into rovings and ready them
for spinning. I know one day he'll leave
the coop. I know he'll be delivered.

THOMAS ARTHUR BROWN

Bought my freedom out of
Maryland and hitched rails into
the ninth concession fencing Chatham.
Married my cupcake, Frances, and
chunked oak wood studs into a sweat-
earned homestead. I river-worked as a
steamboat steward fluking up and down
Old Muddy, flung miles away from my
woodlot tract. Two grey-beard pops
called my kindness, left carpet bags in
my care, and were ghost-absent when
the pigboat stepped away from St. Louis
chuffing down Old Muddy as sunlight
bathed and play-sparkled along the free,
stretched, songline river. Union officers
boarded at Memphis glimming for
contraband. They unravelled the carpet-
bag cargo and I gauped in amazement at
the sight. I was minding Lucifer's
snake sacks, percussion caps destined
for the rebels. I was caught in a hard row
of stumps, mind off, reaching water-well
deep, hauling words to explain I had been
bootleg-screened. Then snug chains landed
on me and I was whisked back to St. Louis

with only work stitches. Now I shammock
back and forth closed in by stone walls,
thinking on my booted family, work-brittle
and alone in Canaan.

OUTSIDE CHATHAM

The forenoon spudges along with sposh
dew dripping down its tow-sack.

I walk past the cradle-knoll dip, searching
for the bister mare's upping block.
Now that Hosea is off soldiering, his tools
play hide-and-go-seek, laying in blackberry,
bramble-bush, or pickney-dragged under
gnarled oak fence-studs.

My mind is work-boiled and all Noah's
creatures say winter will devil us.
Chipping sparrows and skimmers depart early
for southern sun, August fogs cover small
lakes and paint inland meadow streams,
rabbits have fallen like applewood chunks
through the hayloft's mow hole,
the woolly worm's orange bands forthput
flames across fuzzed hatchling backsticks,
and I've never seen more teased wool
forest our border-yard sheep. Through leaf,
pine barren, water, and sky, the lord is
all warning, some horror is readying its time.

READVILLE

I went to flicker the kiln of my calling,
torchlight my name in books I could
barely read, but I'd fallen sick in barracks
before chancing the battle's lead-ball
taste. I hashed all over a thin sheet
pallet and was too gone to clean up
my own vomit. I was drindled and wizzled
to my last run of shad. Smury-headed, I knew my
time was about to go down, and I heard Father
Paul issue my last rites, his voice layered
and speckled, littering the cough-filled room.
Saw heaven's brightest love-light blaring through
a tornado woosh. I was whopper-jawed! Then I was
back in, quicker than a skite second. Opened
my eyes in a snug sink room. Told I was
slapped-out for days and nearly sardined in
a no-count ash-wood box. On the mending
hand, I saw them digging a hole to line
Father Paul: on the cooling board, his eyes
closed, a wind-blown colt's foot scripting his face.

CORNELIUS KING

This is how he saw the world, a line of
tingling notes blown through a bass-clef lens.
They said a musical opened but never closed
in his mind. They called him weed and watched
him grow. One season, tobacco leaves branched
everywhere. The next, boll weevils frosted
green-sea fields, the cracked plants waving lower
each day. The homestead choked through a
dog's dry-bone, fallow summer. His head struggled
to brush the age bar when his brother enlisted,
then his steps pulsed, edging toward the ball's
funnel-line, baby toes fungus-impeached.
If mama had known his endeavor, her tears
would have trenched a valley, coydogs and
her youngest son quicksand-stuck, scrambling
legs in brisk rising water that fathomed dark,
chizzly, and off soundings.

GOSHEN

Mornings, they craunch clove
stems to freshen raffish breath. The buck-
fever, wamble-cropped air swells with
the spiced aroma, humming like a
pawky gadabout through cough-filled halls.
Some are boil-infected, wens lumping
beneath fleshed hulls, singed,
torso hairs gone, many shanks
legs and arms. Around them, serried
bodies cross over simple as breeze-
caressed maple-wood chimes.
Cedar-twig crosses are breeding
in the back-field boneyard.
They can see where the end is headed,
hear it calling their names. The dust dawn
will arrive when even withy-ironed skin,
that endured whiplash, survived
branding, the endless sun-strained
hammermill hours, when that same skin
won't be enough to hold the soul in place.

WAITING

A smoked-fog cloud dress
          roofs our iced-ground

stone-torn feet. Easy
how dusk feeds November

grey through us, as
we watch threshing rains

wallop wind-beaten tents,
dousing the simple breath-

built start-fire smoking through our
tedder-cracked hands. I tell

myself I'm a congress of one, as I
sever kindling branches,

the skinned squirrels, tendon-red and
set for an earth turning

without them. Mud-hen night
          arrives, and our camp exists

outside sound, all voices dried up,
with the brain's dream

winter-still, sparse, and bare-trunked.
I turn sidewise on the

shakedown, lodge quack grass beneath
my rumbled alderman,

my tongue seeking the rainbow feel of
flowing freshets splashed

cold in my bowl-formed daddles.
Dust-filled dawn folds breakfast

smoke cross our mugs, aggravating
the sore-knot fiddling with

my life-stained clackers, tormenting the
nipper that must be chunked

out. Others play cinch with ripped
cards on shuck-bottom

chairs, their mouths frogging round
to stories of their dog-town

kin, pretty doneys, lady bosses, and
      fresh squeakers. Haven't

seen my little woodpiles in months.
      I ease my head against the hay

shock, see clouds rising like chimney-
      smoke scaling the tuned-up sky.

BUCKLE DOWN

I feel like a yard child who's been
cow-kicked and belly-slammed,
but mama says it's my time, as her

kit's youngest, to turn in, take charge,
and man the lead, to pile hayracks,
feed fields with turkey-turd beer,

cope and steer our rawbone herd.
Fair off days I don't mind, and I
can chore hard through full sun

with sharehand skill. I lettuce-feed
biddies as they run through the hen coop,
their papas crowing in morning cold.

I buster and break buckshot soil with
our tag-sale rusted scraper, whaying
the hardhead mule to feist forward.

I grab the oakwood-plow handles tight,
wishing we had a roader horse or anything
else to ease these tush-hog days.

CHAPLAIN

I only knew he'd been lawed for
spying. I listened to his slow words
then spent my news. By noon mark,
his chore time would be done.
We eyed each other, his gaze
fastened to me, his breath and face
chowderhead sozzled. Then his daddles
doddered and tremble-flashed to his toes.
His entirety wind-shook as he snubbed
like a child, salted water flooding all two
sides of his rooter. We set in and prayed,
the lord's book a footlog bridge between us.
They stole him out to meet the knot-knurled
hanging tree, the choker lasso-lit round
his idea-pot. I gaffed onto my rosary beads,
watching him wizzle and subside.
If it be God's will, let it be done.

I have no dry lucifers to prop the fire, so
I take the bow-drill out of my bushcraft
pack and set in with friction to light the
tinder bundle I've fashioned from brittle
leaves and cedar bark, my arms whipped
and played-out, my breadbasket in a huff,
and low-rumbling. The air clouds smoke
round my fists like steam-train puffs.
Two weeks on my own hook and almost
perished that first night. The sheet-iron
crackers vanished faster than daylight.
Raised fool's parsley inches from my lips
before I spied white flowers. Escaped
my demise within a skite second.
I scarf the chipping-squirrel's belly with
my cutter, watch flames lick the insides.
Illuminated, I tuck into the ground-
dweller's tippet and squail bones aside.

CAMP WARD

This is where recruits climbed
the ox-strong span on the branded
shoulders of their seed-folk long
passed, prone in boneyards or
bog-thrown in intervale swampland
to keel up centuries steeped in bondage.

This is where they backed hopes
to the creaking door's dote grain
until apple-shaker winds shivered,
and tamped fires out of them, until falling
weather squeezed through expanded
cedar fissures allowing winter to
dash in full-chisel with its frost mane
ice-hardening mud ground, where straw
beds welcomed critter caravans that
snapped at their exposed flesh.

...and this is where they shoved rags
and knife-hewn hay stalks to mortar
the log wall's daylight-seeking spine
...and this is where some prayed to free
themselves from life's unequal
covenant after upchucking and
throwing out all they had ingested

...and this is where they learned what
doctors knew, that death is a process,
like a sugar tree or wine-glass elm shedding
to its last leaf in put-up flawy winds, how
hearing is the last sense to dissipate

...and this is where their minds angled
home, ribbling off shirttails and
pin-baskets they'd never eye again,
while breathing up-close effects
of consumption, and flu, their coffee-
stained teeth biting the spaces only
sickness fills.

CLATTERING

I was AWOL, an unpaid ridge runner, hawking
distance from the coal-shaded Fifty-fourth
Massachusetts, pulling fleet-foot through night
brush, my feet bramble-clawed and day-sore,
yowling for a pair of spendy cruisers.
Bounty men near caught me in tamarack
larch. I saw their smoothbore guns day clear,
their eyes haired-up and owly. I was hanging
by my eyelids and angled abeam through
light-blazed meadow balm, jumping log cob
and bull stumps, moss-bitten rot-hole fallers,
deploying all the natural speed my buck-bred
seed-folk gave me. I was baseborn in Chatham,
mammy giving life to six pin-baskets in a rickety
pushcart. If I were to see him now, I'd ask daddy
why he heeled-off before eyeing me wrapped in
scrapped yarn. His master named him John, echoing
the New Testament. Whitney's cotton gin nearly snapped
his saddle-brown back in half. Some days he bleated
raw like a crushed side-born calf, sliding away from
full breath. Heard he up and skyrooted through
Virginia pine faster than whiskey jacks whistling
over feed camps, and sparked mammy's teenage
mind before stone-rolling to his novel life, a rail toad
booming around rusted aged jimmys and ragshag

toonerville trolleys. I continued dim-moon travelling
west through puckerbrush, sedge, and prick-filled
tanglewood, lodging with other lucked-out negroes
beside slick calm finger lakes, hauling soaked rick to
hem-load tipcarts. We'd light down to chew tough,
cow-greased pone before snacking tobacco ropes,
our smoky, tea-skinned black bodies day-whipped
and legged out. White clodhopper abolitionists and
schoolmarms let me sleep on shakedowns and boil-up
my battered threads out back, stooped over hose bibbs,
rubboards, or mill-ponds. A swamp Yankee
and his jake-leg wife above Rochester stodged up
scrapple, fire-burnt tunkup, and slack-salted pope's nose.
We popped it down with overproof lamp oil and everyone
was all in, plow-shined. My mind was so jag-skated,
I talked all my closed business like I was up a redwood
tree. Can't extract when my head clunked the sewed-rag
shuck bed. I night-woke bedfast with scarlet runners
beetling my bare flesh. Sweat runnelled and rilled
either side of my chest hillslopes. Heard hushed words
and realized they were studying to mule me to sellers.
Morning I pretended to smile along, then lit
out crow-quick past tumps and shadebark glades of
knurled hickory. On the final night, I met bullhorn
thunderheads throwing froth-smurred gulley washers
and stump-mover skies. I squinched and child-stivered
through teeming chizzly freshets that sozzled and gaffed me,
the mud-water pooling the path's apron. Almost done in,

I saw America's back-forty sproutland, sun-glimming and drying after the rains had sugared-off. I went down the ravine scoop smiling towards birlers and their floaty Niagara chuck boats, waiting to river-cross into Canaan.

THE CRATER

The earth convulsed and refastened
many to the soil from which they were
hatched. The smoothed harrowed ground
plummeted beneath greyback scows,
and two eye-blinks past the din's
dust-mote blare, they occupied a
new juncture, thirty feet under the old,
siege lines and fieldworks gone
like chased rodents. In rising white
smoke, the Yanks missed foot bridges
and became landfill. We were ordered in
and I down-dropped the sump's sliding
pebble slope, ran and log-hopped
bodies impregnating the scarlet, scorched soil,
my eye-blinkers fogged by scowling smoke.
The greybacks rebel-yelled, their right flank
swung like a rusted tin door closing sunlight
and widening the makeshift coffin. Extras
poured in to shore up the bombed split-line.
The turkey-shoot was on. Minie-ball bullets
hammered, bounced backfiring, clacked,
rebounding in the blood-filled dirt bowl.
Negroes domino-fell on all sides of me
and were bayoneted through eyes, last
views looking up, low-angled at the grouty

evil that sentenced them to the reaper's
grim shadow. My body jibed with Solomon's
as we thumped and barrelled to the ground.
I felt more bullets snap behind my backstick
as I gandered at his body beside me, mopboard-still,
and bankrupt of any breathing. I knew I wasn't
going to kick-off, feeling my chest's pluck beat
slow to a crawl. I lay there, silent, making like
I was dead, copying the bung-eyed corpses
spent and spoiling around me.

It's the rebel-yell that rigours chills to
your skillet bones, something the
devil, his own fool self, can't do.
For you, every skirmish line is
amplified to life or death, every
moment is a widow-maker's errand
where your days ravel out, snake-bit,
and you're left with nothing to gaff onto.
The plains-wide absence of surrender
keeps you off-ox, hammer-headed.
Even in jimberjawed, lopsided battles
where the other side overwhelms in
vast numbers, ready to craunch and
rabble your line to bug dust, you must
keep a tush-hog mind.
Union whites can surrender, but no-gimp
negro backouts will be keeled-up and
dispatched to their maker. You know this
sure as you know tomorrow will arrive
with or without you. When the skirmish
is bobbled and your regiment is at its
tag end is when your real fight begins.
You will need to be hell-full ready,
riley, or prepare to bleat weakly like
a lamb before slaughter.

The ship skited full-flank leaning
towards Old Muddy's scrimy tidewater
with the bar-pilot minding us past
where sea and river waters seeded into
each other.

I went under the staysail jib.
The rope-ladder ratlines rattled
above me as I bowsed the bowline.
The barrelman saw their white
anchor-light chained to the growing
wave-filled horizon, the bark's
watermen in the offing.

Their sloop reared-back, geared
against surrender. We set to lick and
pank them good. Our boat lurched
windward, full-chisel pitched over
sagging troughs, like a polished stone
skipped on white-horses foam spraying
the wave tops.

We gained in their afterwash,
our chase-guns hellfilled with chain shot,
cannonballs browsing them broadside.
Their sails flamed sun-yellow like

candle glimstick wicks flared and
whip-cracking the swinged air,
soot smoke billowing.
The rebel ship teetered a tumbleset
before she capped and turtled under.

FORT PILLOW MASSACRE

We had long soured on fortune's
prompt arrival, reinforcements
scarce as hen's teeth,
as we faced bullet-laden tides
firing shotgun grapeshot
that never turned.
No prayer could dampen the
heavy buckshot blare of canister
rounds tumbling in over log banking,
my sightlines smoke-blurred,
lead minies pock-marking the
piled log-wood barrier.
The gatlings levelled men in fives.
Outgunned and hilled-in
we hollered calf-rope
and grafted white shirts
to poles and branch sticks,
anything resembling surrender.

Happened on a moment after
the firing closed, and we knew
our surrender was revoked.
Their eyes glared gunmetal,
lead-cold Confederate grey.
Jupiter was the first to drop,

point-blank begging for quarter.
Then the colonel's voice
cracked stone before he dispatched
more to quell their quaking.
Said no niggah should evah fiah
on a Southerner. The captured Yanks
begged them to grant us quarter.
Then bullets yaggered from all sides.
Southerners butchered us in holes,
their bayonets scooping both eyes,
blood squalling down cheek-lines.
Slaughtered two more cowering
in the smoke house, their feet tasted
Big Muddy's ambling water.
I lay devoid of motion
with a dead man's bloodied brain
splattered on my shirt, trying hard
to fence my breathing.

GRAND JUNCTION

I became contraband,
nearabout muled back to bondage
when a copperhead and his consort
let me night in their hayloft,
but I heard him wish General Lee
had triumphed in Antietam,
and closed the ball early. I had to
acknowledge the corn before
he grabbed his pig sticker.
I fleet-footed for miles through
torn Tennessee, hitched with fellow
runners ploughing north on holed
wagon roads. We reached Union lines
where pickets led us under spry
moon gleam. We wolfed down
livermush before sips of old red-eye
laid us log-still. Morning splashed the
Jonahs' den we had happened into.
Scores of fellow negroes lay strewn
with their heads balanced on haversacks,
some greyback-infected, filled with
pipjennies, slumped with shakes on litters.
The strong rooted up for coloured regiments.
They were tenderfoot fresh fish
fitted in Northern navy wool sack-coats,

cupping lead pill boxes and shooting irons.
There were top-rail sawbones employing
keen mother-wit in the field hospital.
Near mustered-out Yanks arrived
like fallen timber, prone on pushcarts,
others shanks' mare. It was like butcher's fare.
Sawbones wallpapered the wounded
with pop-skull whiskey before severing
limbs clean through joints, the sliced
screams ear-cracking sharp like
chain lightning crisping pealed flesh.

NEW YORK DRAFT RIOTS

The Irish-bogtrotters were up-in-arms
dogged as they stormed sweltering
streets like a bat cloud or a swift murder
of carrion crows gutting dead field cows,
the riotous mass sweeping all corners
and the hide-places of gadabouts, buzzwigs,
and any bad-off, blue-gum negro they could find.
They rammed up Manhattan's fire-and-tow
stone roads, carrying brickbats, shovel scoops,
and hardwood bludgeons. The ragtag mob trimmed
fussed-up hundred-dollar-men, tore sparkled
gewgaws straight off bystander wrists,
emptied pockets clean, and stripped
them of their clothing, whistle britches,
drawers and all. Those who managed
escape were so whipped and wopsed
their talk was skimble-scambled, like fresh
paplaps recently fetched from their mothers'
wombs. Coffee-shaded porters were clouted
and flattened dead or within inches of their
time. The soused rabble, then over a thousand
fortified, were scraped from the charcoal-
burnt, infernal, coal-smoldering pit of hell.
Hummed-up, they moved like a raving flood.
It was judgement day for the innocent and

lord-fearing. Porting iron bars, they swarped
known white republicans, grabbed an on-duty
blue bottle and pelted him like a rag doll
into a rubble pile, ensuring his end run. Then
the bogtrotter rats set in on negroes, hanging
one from a blooded lamppost so those behind
could express further outrage by gutting the
knife-holed corpse. The day continued on the
down go, as they flash-flooded 5th Avenue to
the Coloured Orphan Asylum, kyoodling
"burn the niggers' nest," and crashed through
the hack-broken front door, then set into
tear planking as women hushed children out the
hindmost scuttle-door under schoolmarm aprons,
while older woodpiles backed smaller pin-baskets
striking out the rear exit as the crowd uprooted
paving stones and launched them against the
little shirttails attempting to flee. The mob
clunked and pocked the building's
heated-brick walls, splintering windows,
the rising smoke blackening smudged sills,
Outside the entrance, a yard child lay silent
beneath a dresser the riley boodle had flung on her.
They grabbed and smashed play-pretties, cribs,
baby buggies, washed diapers, and set flame to
any furniture-suit blocking their way. They
grabbled and pulled a tar-shaded coachman,
roping him through the streets by his privates.

No bark-shaded cartmen could move
fast enough to skite out and ditch the hayfork
and firewood-toting ragtag rabble. All over,
negroes were bushed-up behind doors or in
hidey holes, ascared of the deepening low dark.
The orphaned woodpiles were barged on the
East River, listening to the smoldered sky sizzle,
their night and childhood translated to flames.

LATCHING BLACKBIRDS

Landsmen all, we manned barks,
sloops, and schooners in Lincoln's
blue-water fleet, enforcing our martial
blockade on the rebels' deep-harbour portsteps.
I roped burned rigging through calloused hands,
ran between berth and gun decks,
feeding whites with gunpowder boxes.

When the blackbirding ship rose
onto our rolling pearl-foamed horizon,
we waited for the lookout's signal.
The gunners readied, eyes moored
on the intruder's sail-path.
I grabbed my pepperbox and clocked
the trigger, awaiting a dog-scrap growl.
They reached our vanguard, and captain
squawked "avast!" while our fingers
skimmed the hair trigger.

Old bondage bark, three-masted, chain-loaded
with live cargo. Negroes fetched from rootland
sands quiled down on slave-deck planking,
jawing in rhythmic tongues,
pagan, god-withdrawn in nakedness,
spent and massed like netted krill.

The whites stealing them old scratches
from hell's bowels, hands hiked for quarter.
The hold harboured crying pickneys,
anchored in their own roiling mess spread
like molasses burnt beneath them.
Their parents and I scoped eyes at each other,
the distance measured in upturned centuries,
crimped and moribund, a Saragasso sky eaten by clouds.

BLOCKADE

They're trying to buy
the sea's silence from shore,
stuff its mouth dry with ballast
as surging channel waves
rummage stone harbour-walls.

John Bull's British sloops want to
touch shore with wave-breezed sails,
but we've girdled cotton docks
tighter than skin on bones. Bales
are piled-up and overwhelm harbour
planking. All those bundles turned
to mould-filled decay, heavy-wet
and sawyer-beetle-infected.

Klatches of men sit sozzled, others
stand yelling in chewing matches.
A couple well-placed lit lucifers,
will tear New Orleans open like a
pulled cornhusk revealing the
sweet kernels, ripe and set to eat.

INTRUDER IN THE DUST

I've been leadball-fumbled,
the grapeshot bits pinning me
to this fallow field.

I try to gain the cradle knoll,
my arms outstretched.
I grip needlegrass, try to pull
myself to the slash fence,
my daddles in full break,
useless as cotton leafworms.

Either it's fixin to rain,
or greyback cannons have
hummed up and creeped in closer.
Everwho remains from our spade
regiment, are screaming
from all the metal bits
tunnelling through them.
I'm cat-fit clinging to life
with each in-breath.
In slow deliberation, the days
are coming to collect me.

CAPTURED

Can't believe this spalt-wood, patched
hay barrack, filled with other failed-up
skillet troops, some as young as shirttails,

is my current stay place. Nights, I try to reach
back through shudders, see my tacker self
holding mama's tedder-worked hands, dry hay

flecks devilling her palms. I now know hunger
is the loudest sound. Befriended a Kentucky
corn-cracker who later tried to flee. Plott hounds

shredded him to meat chunks. They found
his eye and sun-dried brown-skin in a small
mushroom grove edging the corduroy road.

Reports from the ball's shell-torn frontlines
reveal pokerish horror, calamity, and devilled
injustice edging soldier and civilian.
We give warning, right followers of Abraham
might become heavy-sick from this flat truth.
Man and horse have been cannon-blown to bits,
left dying in dogwood meadows, bayonet-impaled,
goat-bled between houses, in barns, haylofts,
forlayed in makeshift bone-orchards.
Antietem, Shiloh, Spotsylvania, Court House,
Chickamauga, and Gettysburg, each
one dwarfing Napoleon's Waterloo.

Negro troops are Job-burdened, receiving no
quarter. Confederate potlickers have massacred
negroes who've surrendered their eveners and
mud-splotched rusted revolvers. Negro hides
are found wizzled, laying side by each in
willywags, fly-infected twitch grass, yellowed
coltsfoot, and skinned in fraid holes. Negroes
aiming to jump in the broil, desiring to unlatch
their bonded brethren, are urged to backen,
hobble their voices and review their steps!

FRENCH LEAVE

I'm on dogwatch
drafting my eyes through
frayed water, wave-packed,
the ocean bounds decks, eddies,
soaks the forward-facing pivot-guns.

I serve without commission
while my salary drindles.
I don't want to go on the prod
planting rippets with our sass-box
skipper, or crab to the Yankee blue
jackets, who are all beat-out,
and deaf to negro bellyaches.

Months gale round flap sails.
I am dropping stones
with shakes and quick-step,
my stomach fires and falls back,
the rib lines pronounced
beneath my shirt.

When we make homeport,
and whites go down the line,
me and Jobah will hoof it
through bubby bush and pine breaks,

suggin sacks slapped to our shirtbacks,
hoping for abolitionist hovels.
When we daylight to Niagara swells,
we'll hitch cut sourwood, arriving
in Upper Canada no-poke penniless,
ready to tell our betters how Yanks
gaffled and tolled us, hoping we'd
be backwoodser goosecaps.

THE FORAGERS

Above the mud-bank butt
and through the fence-lined field,
they're progging. They graze to
the spring house after the missus
fetches her words. She tries to
push them on. How their eyes
trample potatoes and carrot tops
as their sun-dried mud hands
separate flapping witch grass and
cow-corn stacks.

Skipjacks flicker silver sparks
above the swift river line.
The creek chub are finally
bulking the buck net, where winds
cat-paw the water's snug hem to
the wheedled hours flourishing
shadows over scrimy water.

The thunder dog-growl fusses
my squeezed stomach-keg's walls.
Some of us are already spleeny
and rawbone brickle, crowbait
thinned to the ledge of harm.

I piroot and see them skew up
the hill slope, over maiden cane,
fallfish swinging from skillet-
black hands, fired coffin nails
flagpoled in their mouths,
aired up and blaring.

RICHMOND

We crossed the bridge into Richmond,
arrowing towards the centre with
negro throngs shawled around us.
They massed like quickwater and ocean-waved
at the foot of Jefferson Davis' mansion.
I wish I had seen the evil tumblebug
pull-foot and skite away.
I tag-tailed other burrheaded skillets,
and we duffed down on a lumber
wagon as it creeped forward, aided
by the addition of our weight.
The grey rebels were in their
last day of shad, their lines elderly,
belly-slammed, and fushed out.
Everything was on the gain.
Children whirled tumblesets on the
soft and over-fussed beardgrass, their
shoeless feet cow-kicking victory vees.
Others had searched the tacker chambers
and sat with play-pretties under moss-
branched pin oaks. White folks cut-eyed us,
shamefaced and hangdogged, even the
women were forked, their brows bushed-up
and riley. I was handed squirrel whiskey
which I elbow-bent and flickered down

in a wink. The stump-water fire rivered from
my keg to the tips of my daddles. I choired
with the kyoodling tunket till night blinked out.

TAKING CHARLESTON

We walked unopposed into
the ball's cradle, smelling and
seeing the first-class devastation
our shelling had authored.
Negroes cheered and popped out
from gutted stone churches, dirt-pit
abodes, clinging to fresh-pine abatis,
or emerged from under cracked
canvas in cloth-sewn roadside tents.

We moved horse-gallop fast,
tightening neighbourhoods like a
screw, fly-swatting leftover rebels
crow-perched on rooftops, or
lone-firing out open windows.
We were in constant motion,
the hours kedging away from us.

Our cracker-line extended while
doughballs, hard-tack, and corn trace
continued to roll in. Greyback paddies
over-armed stones as we marched by.
On harbour road, I saw our heavy cruisers
fill up the port's choppy mouth,
an announcement pounding the
black-rubboard-road's gravel chat.

FORT WAGNER

They crawled across
sun-scorched beach sand,
clambering beneath cannonball
bombardment blazing from the
fort's stone brow.
The burnt, sour-egg,
sulphur reek flowed into their
rooters as the shoreline convulsed
with each smoothbore cannon-blast.

Men spilled into eternity's
tide-hole in the sloped, quivering
ground hulled around them,
bullets chunked up idea
pots like a dull grubbing hoe.
Every ear-blast boomer wail
presented cutglass-sharp,
heated metal shrapnel tickets to
the breath's sapped tag-end,
the ego's clear pith
repaired to that sky home from
where we all come.

INTO THE
BONEYARD

ANDERSONVILLE PRISON

Guards peel men like rot-sore
onions with bullwhip lashes
targeting bare-flesh turns of skin,
wherever the branding rod can
fire-burn and shoulder-sign the
body's crisp arm rotators.

Some are giving up on themselves.
They pig together in penned areas,
the lucky on log scoots,
their minds hulled and browsed,
some in loud-sleep, roaring
thunder snores. Others are
bull's-eyed to the freedom of
still-footed smoke trees,
yards beyond the slash fence
and stone-row milk gap.

FIELD CAMP

We're setting a place for death.
Every time a sneeze erupts I pull lapels
to hug my yap, feel humid summer planting

fungus in my toe pits. How long can we play
cinch and hang by our eyelids, surrounded by
scrimy walls, knowing each inhaled breath

carries the backdoor trot sending us out to
squat over turd-filled needlegrass or smoothed
wood-planking over dug-holes, our stomachs

wizzled and scythe-cut. Our lives circle
the general's focal point. The urge to live here
perishes as each day tongues over the hills.

My live luck tired in Nashville,
there, where the river shoehorned,
drawing sloped mud banks within
stone-skipping distance. My wallowed
innards tumbled down through my keg.

I knew midnight's cloaked
scamp had come to summon me
and I quilled my last will and testament,
scrawled on ripped poke paper hand-
loaned to me by a button backwoodser.

Discharged the homestead and land's
residue to my sugar-faced lady, Hardinia,
twenty-five top milk-acres resting in
Kent county where yieldy soils breathe in
the endless lake-water drisk. Further on,
if the afore-mentioned dropped off into a
scented pine box, I bequeathed all to my
flowering pin-basket, Mary, latched
in bondage, praying she'd run the ridge
and reach safety, gaffle all upcountry
rich tract that's rightfully hers.
This be my last will and testament.

MARY FIELDS

She grabbed massa's book-bent
daguerreotype showing her, Jericho,
and the rape-bred brood standing in
the slave house's peppertree shade.
She absquatulated with the foundling
and two other brown pin-baskets
and outstepped the day's burnt leather
leash. Night winds unroofed slate-cloud
rain-piles crackling apple-shaker boomers
as they slept on raw ginned cotton padding
heaped inside an abolitionist's closed hayloft.
They morning-rose with budding May colour
stippled across oaks and benched stolid in
dank undergrowth which carried itself away
from homestead steps, past the horse feed-
bunk, out to a cut-timber corduroy road,
leading to where barn-high father Lincoln's
word begat freedom and cinched slaves' lives.
They downed smother with red flannel hash.
How her children painted bread in beet juice,
her fork stuck in doughballs and tuckahoe,
everyone's eyes waiting till the roiled afternoon
heat sundered, and the north star awakened,
showing the cow's-tail path, which they
would follow, come freedom or demise.

AND THERE SHE MINISTERS

They back hope to men horse-carted
in from the frontline's smurry thunder-
stone conveyor belt, soldiers' arms flopping
out the basket wagon, teeth bite-clenched
on buggy traces— or arm-broke bleeding,
painting chained whippletrees red.
Shiners lie squandered all through
the field fever shed, flat on haybeds,
piles of severed limbs a refuse
tump slabbed beside them, many
horse-sensed enough to know their rain
barrels are on the down go.

They hand amputation-saws over to
sawbones, and crosstie tourniquets,
and shirttail fabric-dams trying to hold
the red in. Queer how the new
bullets shimmer-glimmer like a tacker's
play-pretties: spiralling in flight, they
snap bones clean, tunnelling through
the body's wet tissue-layers, the way a
knife never could. Benumbed, these
deathbed Eves see life thin to the buzz
folded in mosquito nets, see its last
gibble-gabble ahead of evenfall.
They note each time they see the reaper's

pop call, cunning, homing to feed
the foot-pocked dusted ground from
whence we all came.They reckon the body
is always at war, always set-in against itself,
like a country trying its best to stand, with
one foot low-sick and plagued with contagion,
the other shoeless, hobbling into tomorrow.

BANNER

Woodsborn rustic hayseeds stand
eyeing the negro scores turkey-
trotting the valley's pebble ribbon,
blue infantry stripes paced
in unison, steps equal in footfalls,

the odd vision hay-scratching
their oxblood-red eyes,
view of a cotton-ball century
donkey-carting away from them.

Arrowing towards Savannah,
coloured soldiers carry the seeds
of a new nation rooting rich
inside their idea pots.

The flag-man's streamer
wind-waves at barnfowl clucking
and plocking bits of clod under
the pignut and slash-pine bowery.

The regiment hums up,
heads balcony-high and
forthputting, as if their reaching
daddles could touch and
smooth the moon's surface.

THE BLACK UNION DEAD

The sun-shattered morning light sieves
through bottomlands illuminating cadavers
rippled under the trees' tea-green antlers.
Me and Abel bend low,
hinge, and shoulder remains from
the Tennessee's mud-soaked banks.

Their arms fall like cut branches
dragged through thickets. They land
with dampened thuds, blood-smudging
the others roped and tagged.
Stink rot is moored everywhere,
from scarred battlefield skirmish lines
to no-count dog towns, bodies gas-bloated,
maggot-gnawed, decayed swill for
scavenging pot-bellied hogs belching
their fill.

When the deceased
mirror our hickory-bark shade,
we pause, cripple flickering seconds,
our shovels spearing fathoms of earth.

AFTERMATH

The broke-rock ground is
tumbled-down thunder.
We're off-loading shiners
by their stone-still legs.

Even God can't wade in
water no more. An old
bewhiskered pop is trembling
on the roadside's lip, his
brown fists shanking the
ripped earth as if Jesus
made his first mistake.

I myself am rigged to buck-pile
corpses, incensed at all this
injustice feeding boneyards.
How days tick, edging
life forward inside us.

Child-traced
in s q u i g g l y pencil line,

        the   sun

      s   e
        m i l

t
u
 m
  b
  l
   e
    s

    on corpse-strewn fields
bordering the shuck house
and stump ranch.

Corn stalks continue their ascent,
silk tendril fronds

                    f

                 a

                  l

             l

                    on a leg less
                         buffalo soldier

the husk's teeth
yellowing into summer
                    as if nothing has happened.

Even this perfect day with
no brickle clouds continues
its steady march towards midnight hands,
kneels in wisteria pollen,
hears crickets sounding July.

How it leans into itself,
it's hourglass patterns shredded
with light.
How the land they cashed-in for
continues without them,

how the body is
a vessel with no escape.

Waves of tufted twitch grass clutch
them the way a beggar might, all strength
and no chance of
             letting go.

How the ground brings
its ultimate angleworm appetite.

GEORGE M. LUCAS

He made it through Burden's Causeway,
survived the deadfall shelling and
helped rebuild the burned-down bridge,
making it stouter than before.

Came news his bedrid wife had let
go of life's hitching-strap back in
sweet-tree Niagara, leaving their five
tackers reft motherless and burdened
onto others not blood-matched to them.
He was granted furlough, and rushed
back from blue-granite Carolina.
Trains split the wind at full chisel,
steel cog-wheels pirooting like
released south-born twisters
crosstied to rust-brown rail lines.

George had to right the world in
thirty days, brace each plank side
and provision his shirttails with care,
his mind dirt-thrown and unbalanced
like a broken plow. Days later,
he found himself in the sandlapper state
dodging rifle-pit fire, only to be
flaked under a sweep-willow's arms,

his small pickneys up north
anxious for his pop-call knock,
the two young buttons with faces
pinned to window glass,
unaware he wasn't coming.

BURIAL DUTY

They give the moment
the spiritual it needs,
their harmonies overlapping
hours, the dirge resonant.

Daily, they see time has
its own scripture, pens its
own lines and preaches from
the most profound beholden
gospel, the dead planked,
arms and feet over-spilling
the carriage bed.

The man-mess spreads
through the dropping-filled
chicken yard, a detached,
crusted head stares back,
gapmouthed, clumped skin
rotting, in-turned eye-torches
snuffed-out. Behind the barn,
buzzards battle for a greyback's
forearm. They've fetched it
through its fabric house and
clawed the sun-broiled flesh.

They turn in and buckle
down, iron-shovels hard-ground
rubbling. They lay the stiff
cadavers side-by-each,
the roiling reek fastened
in their patched overalls.

Nights they light glimsticks,
crack open ground-nuts
and pack tales beside
spill-pines. When they lie out
they hear whippoorwills and
nightjars trill, their splayed
feet pottering and skipping
through crackerberry
and swale brush.

CONSUMPTION

Haven't seen or felt a battle scrap,
and here I am mind-dragging each
moment to its own eternity, severely
on the down-go. I know I'm all in.

My eyes clench into the
fabric of these field-hospital walls,
the horrid, severed-pig-head,
blood-squealing cries saying
we're all refundable.

Flower-filled with tumbling feathers,
I think the blue jays and side swallows
know winter is coming earlier this year.
My breath is well past its flowering,
the voice gone to pasture. The life
I've composed is nearly sugared-off.

I'm a memory-filled basket
turned on its side. Knowing the
future is not the same as knowing
what will happen. I can see the glow-
winged threshold yee-yawed
to the night, hear my childhood
voice ask, "is you ready?"

BREAKFAST

Hovered over fried creek chub,
men listen to the incoming
blast blare boom
shredding the air's hem like
a breaking plow bustering
the earth's ground bone.

Men belly-slammed and tumbleset
with a roar like gush-water bursting
through the levee boil.

A couple three were able to rear
up and glim the sky's eye burning
them, their earholes gathering the
death-wail of the snuffed out, now

blood seeding the grey clunched soil,
uniforms turned to underlay,
a cushion for their last
stay place.

JAMES JONES

Table candles burn like my youth's call-light,
yawning brightness through this gathered
spalt-wood hen shack. I joined the 55th Mass
cavalry barely old enough to squirrel corn
whiskey and had no duds nor sawbucks to shine
a lady boss. When recruiters gave out word
seeking dogtown snowballs and pluck negroes
to turn in, I joined and set myself hard, buckled
down to my heart-cob. I bundled wudgets, ricked
wood, and never battle-fled like yellow-bellied
backouts. I felt gaffed and top-turned when I
was mustered out sans ceremony. I spent two
crocked years dodging disease and coiled gun-
spun minies, and no cent crawled its way to
my wrinkled, tended-out mitts. Now I
wane in full fail-up, waiting for boodle to
pension through, another runt day thrown
in the ditchline.

THEATRE

It feels as if the ground is grease-fried
and welded with thunder, news-mortared
and made brickle by words of most ill-fortune.
My mind can't tender a greater calamity.
Everyone, from wood ticks and appleknockers
to upstreet paps, is hewn to the last
page of stubbed-up silence. Booth has taken
the sun. My feet are another's feet and I don't
know how to drive them. Even the air feels
two-ton and inflamed. I see seasoned women
bawling, stalled in the gravel road's passway.
Men are riled and grouty, a logline of fused faces,
corked, fronting yellow hay tipcarts. I myself am
rigged with a clipped, hacked ticker, incensed and
pine-needled by injustice, and they say Massa
Lincoln, our own Massa Lincoln, he dead.

GLOSSARY

Absquatulate – take leave, disappear

Alderman – stomach, big stomach

Appleknocker – travelling farmhand

Backstick – back/backlong

Ball – war/battle

Barrelman – sailor stationed in the crow's nest

Beholden – owing gratitude, indebted

Bister – yellowish-brown

Blackbirding – kidnapping people to work as slaves

Boneyard – cemetery

Bowse – to pull or haul

Breadbasket – stomach

Brickle – brittle

Buck – log pile

Bumbershoot – umbrella

Burrheaded – having tightly-curled hair

Buster – plow, breaking plow

Butt – ridge that stands out prominently from
surrounding area

Button – young, inexperienced man

Buzzwhig – big shot

Calf-rope – surrender

Chat – gravelly tailings

Chist – bag

Chizzly – chilly and damp

Chowderhead – idiot

Clackers – teeth

Clodhopper – awkward person

Clunch – hardened clay, chalky limestone

Coffin nail – cigarette

Coltsfoot – perennial with yellow flowers

Coonjine – rhythmic gait for loading freight

Copperhead – Northerner with Southern sympathies

Coydog – hybrid between coyote and wild dog

Cracker line – supply line for troops on the move

Cradle knoll – mound with a cradle-like depression
     next to it

Craunch – chew noisily, crush

Crocked – crazy

Daddles – hands

Deacon – learn, acquire through knowledge

Dog watch – a short watch period

Dog-town – poor section of town

Drindle – weaken, diminish, waste away

Drisk – drizzle

Duds – clothing

Evenfall – the onset of evening

Fallfish – freshwater fish

Fire and tow – excitable

Flake – dead

Fluking – sailing

Footlog – log serving as a bridge

Forenoon – morning

Forked – violent

Foundling – abandoned infant

Fraid hole – cave

Free stall – dairy barn

French leave – to go absent without leave

Fush out – fail, die

Fuss up – dress up

Gadabout – drifter

Gaffle – cheat, swindle

Gibble-gabble – senseless chatter

Glim – a look/glimpse; a lamp/lamplight

Glimstick – candle

Go on the prod – irritable, offensively angry

Goosecap – fool

Greybacks – lice, derogatory term for
    Confederate soldiers

Gulley washer – heavy rain

Hammer-headed – stubborn

Hangdog – ashamed, unhappy

Hantle – crowd

Hayseed – unsophisticated person

Hitching strap – the connection between a
    wagon/buggy and a horse

Idea-pot – head

Intervale – low-lying land

Jawing – talking

Jib – foremost frontward triangular sail

Jimberjawed – protruding, lopsided lower jaw

Kedge – to drift

Keel-up – kill

Knot – a swelling, lump; a boil.

Lady boss – wife

Maiden cane – large grass

Milk gap – opening where cows are let in for milking

Minie balls – deadly advanced bullets used in Civil War

Minies – minie ball bullets

Mow hole – opening in hayloft floor for throwing down hay

Mud hen – black-crowned night heron

Nipper – tooth

Off soundings – out of one's depth, in deep water

Owly – angry

Paddy – woman, tramp

Pap – grandfather

Paplaps – babies

Pawky – sneaky, sly

Pepperbox – multiple-barrel revolver

Pigboat – lake steamship

Pignut – hickory chair that bears nuts with thin husks

Pin-basket – child

Pip jenny – pimple

Piroot – whirl around

Play-pretty – toy

Plocking – a short, low clicking sound

Poke – money pouch

Pop – grandfather

Pop-call – unexpected visit

Pope's nose – rump of a cooked fowl

Potlicker – contemptible person

Progging – foraging

Puckerbrush – land with scrub brush

Quarter – surrender

Quick-step – diarrhea

Quile down – settle down

Rawbone – bony

Ribble-off – recite by rote

Rick – wood bundle

Riley – angry

Rippet – fight, noisy disturbance

Rooter – nose

Rubboard – unpaved road

Runnel – a small stream

Sandlapper – someone from South Carolina

Sawbones – surgeon

Scow – large foot

Scrimy – dirty, stingy

Scrog – damage

Seed-folk – ancestors

Serry – packed crowd

Shammock – walk in a shambling or idle way

Shanks – without

Shiner – black person

Shirttail – boy, child; small amount

Skew – suddenly change direction

Skimble-scamble – rambling and confused, senseless

Skimmer – bird that skims the water

Skipjack – fish that leaps above the water

Skite – leave quickly, to hurry

Skyroot – fast, go quickly

Sloop – small warship

Smurry – hazy, cloudy, overcast

Snowball – poor white person

Sozzle – idle, splash

Spalt – decayed wood

Spill pine – needle pine

Spleeny – sickly

Sposh – mud

Sproutland – land covered with saplings

Spudge along – mosey along

Squeaker – child

Stiver - stagger

Stoneboat – sled for transporting stones

Stone-row – stone fence

Stub-up – uncooperative, sullen

Stump-mover – heavy rain

Sugar off – to finish off, bring to a conclusion

Swale – low-lying tract of land, meadow

Swamp Yankee – old fashioned rural New Englander

Swarp – to beat

Swinged – singed, burnt

Swoo – cow/cow call

Tacker – child, tyke

Tag sale – sale of used household items

Ticker – heart

Tippet – rump

Toonerville trolley – rundown or unreliable railcar, trolley, etc.

Trill – quavering warbling sound

Trim – to beat

Tumblebug – dung-rolling beetle

Tumbleset – somersault

Tump – small hill, clump of marshy vegetation

Tumpline – headstrap used to ease the weight of a load carried on the back

Tunket – an informal party

Tunkup – mashed potatoes

Turkey-turd beer – fertilizer made of water and manure

Tush hog – tough, aggressive person

Underlay – something placed under or beside something else

Up a tree – drunk

Upping block – mounting block

Wamble-cropped – sick

Wen – lump or swelling under the skin

Whay – command to a cow

Whippletree – part of a wagon attaching the horse

Whook – call to animals

Willywag – underbrush

Withy – strong, wiry

Wizzle – weaken, shrivel up, die

Wopse – wollop, beat

Wudget – bundle

Yee-yawed – askew

ACKNOWLEDGEMENTS

I'm indebted to Bryan Prince and his excellent book, *My Brother's Keeper: African Canadians and the American Civil War*. I'm equally indebted to Richard M. Reid for his book, *African Canadians in Union Blue: Volunteering for the Cause in the Civil War*.

Eternal gratitude to the editors of the publications in which some of these poems have appeared, sometimes in different form:

Best Canadian Poetry in English 2018, EnRoute magazine, Exile Quarterly, Freefall, and *The Walrus*.

My complete gratitude to the judges of the 2016 CBC Poetry contest for selecting "African Canadian in Union Blue" as the winning poem. The judges were Roo Borson, George Elliott Clarke, and Erín Moure.

Thanks to the following people for their advice, time, and support: Karri Hutchinson, Nathalie Paquet, Luke Hathaway, Erika Sanborn, Vanessa Stauffer, Emily Donaldson, Dan Wells, Dulce Felix, Maria Carnevale, James Deahl, Carmela De Luca, Tara Haas, Bernadette Forsyth, Margherita Carducci, Ildikó Nagy, Ruth Roach Pierson, Molly Peacock, Khadijah Jabari, Heather Wood, Jim Nason, Jean King, Myna Wallin, Charlene Diehl, Barbara Schott, Dane Swan, Carmine Starnino, Krystyna Wesolowska, Silvia Franzoi, Donna Badgley, Brittany Tomin, Darryl Bank, Sadiya Mirza, Sarah Ignaczewski, Yanny Zhang, Sonya Ben-Ishai,

Alexia Vuckovic, Nicole Landry, Pablo Garcia, Fauzya Alarakhia, Monique Twigg, Davis Sessions, and Michael Stanislaus.

Thanks to the Plasticine Poets: Charlie Petch, Lisa Young, Kate Flaherty, Lisa Richler, Susie Berg, David Clink, Rod Weatherbie, Mary Rykov, Dave Noel, Robin Richardson, Lizzie Violet, and Phoebe Tsang.

Copious thanks to the Toronto Arts Council, Ontario Arts Council, and Canada Council for the Arts.

PHOTO: MICHELLE KOLTONOV

MICHAEL FRASER is published in various national and international journals and anthologies. His manuscript *The Serenity of Stone* won the 2007 Canadian Aid Literary Award Contest and was published by Bookland Press in 2008. He is published in *Best Canadian Poetry in English 2013* and *2018*. He has won numerous awards, including *Freefall Magazine*'s 2014 and 2015 poetry contests, the 2016 CBC Poetry Prize, and the 2018 Gwendolyn Macewen Poetry Competition. *The Day-Breakers* is his third book of poems.